CRYPTOCURRENCY MINING

The Complete Guide to Mining Bitcoin, Ethereum and other Cryptocurrency

by

Devan Hansel

© 2017 Devan Hansel

All rights reserved. No part of this book may be reproduced in any form without permission in writing from the author. Reviewers may quote brief passages in their reviews.

Disclaimer

No part of this publication may be reproduced or transmitted in any form or by any means, mechanical or electronic, including photocopying or recording, or by any information storage and retrieval system, or transmitted by email without permission in writing from the publisher.

While all attempts have been made to verify the information provided in this publication, neither the author nor the publisher assumes any responsibility for errors, omissions, or contrary interpretations of the subject matter herein.

This book is for entertainment purposes only. The views expressed are those of the author alone, and should not be taken as expert instruction or commands. The reader is responsible for his or her own actions.

Adherence to all applicable laws and regulations, including international, federal, state, and local governing professional licensing, business practices, advertising, and all other aspects of doing business in the US, Canada, or any other jurisdiction is the sole responsibility of the purchaser or reader.

Neither the author nor the publisher assumes any responsibility or liability whatsoever on the behalf of the purchaser or reader of these materials.

Any perceived slight of any individual or organization is purely unintentional.

Get the FREE Bonus NOW!

If you're interested in receiving free PDFs on latest strategies, guides and secret tips about topics like cryptocurrency, bitcoin, blockchain, online trading, investing, real estate, stock market etc., I highly recommend you to join my list (link below) I've spent many years understanding all this stuff and I will provide you the distilled knowledge that can not only save you hundreds of hours but also thousands of dollars. Members in my list essentially get to learn how to make money and invest it wisely. To Subscribe, go to the link below.

www.bit.ly/devan-hansel

As a bonus, members will also be getting my latest books for FREE before anyone else. Yes, FREE. However, this is an exclusive invite and will expire soon. It doesn't cost you anything to join. You will only have to put in your email-id so that I can connect with you and keep you updated. It's a clear win-win. So, go ahead and subscribe now by visiting the link: www.bit.ly/devan-hansel

Note to the Readers

First off, I'd like to commend you for actually following up on your curiosity and getting this book. Given the public interest and rising market valuation of cryptocurrencies, this book is definitely a smart and timely purchase. The value of cryptocurrencies has skyrocketed since their inception back in 2009 with Bitcoin. A window of opportunity has opened up for those who are interested enough to learn and brave enough to venture. Make no mistake, there is a lot of wealth to be made in this field. 2 years from now, people will look back and wonder why they didn't get on the boat while they still had the chance. The fact that you've bought this book indicates your interest. But are you willing to seize the opportunity?

A lot of time and effort has gone into creating the book you are now reading. And I sincerely hope that it helps you move ahead in your quest for useful knowledge. The book has been designed to take you gradually through the hoops and introduce the cryptocurrency investing landscape, one block at a time. As such, care has been taken to ensure that anybody can read and understand the material without too many prerequisites. The book has also been written in a short-and-concise format to allow readers to flip through the book quickly. However, if you happen to find it difficult at times, please go through the resources recommended within the context. Good Luck!

About the Author

Hi there! I am Devan Hansel. I'm a crypto-investor and cat lover. Over the years, I've acquired a wide range of experiences in investing and the art of money-making. I've been involved in the stock market, real estate, tech startups and more recently…cryptocurrencies and blockchain. Having studied computer science and finance in college, I could easily grasp the essence of the technology and understand how the whole system works. In this book, I've laid out all the essential knowledge you need to understand to start tapping the market and make profitable investments quickly. I've put my maximum effort in making it interesting and understandable. I hope you have a good time reading the book :)

Come join my list if you want to follow latest trends in the marketplace and get huge discounts on early releases of my books. All you need to do is enter your email-id in the link below so that I can communicate with you about my latest works and keep you in the loop.

www.bit.ly/devan-hansel

Why You Should Read This Book

If you're interested in capturing wealth then the cryptocurrency market is undoubtedly the #1 place to go to right now. Millionaires are being made in a matter of months. This is a fact. There are two kinds of people who are making money in the crypto space. The investors and the miners. If you're not in possession of the investment capital or the knowledge of essential investment strategies, you need not worry. Cryptocurrency Mining is an option that will deliver you the same (or more) results if you know how to do it right.

To help you decide, let me elaborate more. Here are the factors that make cryptocurrency mining a sensible option.

1. **Cryptocurrencies are decentralized.** That means, no single financial organization or hedge fund can control the stock value or use market manipulation tricks. The power is with the public. And the technology that supports this open decentralized framework is called Blockchain which will be covered in chapter-2.

2. **The market is super young.** The first cryptocurrency, Bitcoin, was released in 2009 and trading cryptocurrencies picked up steam around 2012-2013. So, it's only around 5-6 years old. Very small percent of the global population is even aware of cryptocurrencies and even smaller percent knows how to make profits from them. So, the chances for capturing a piece of the pie are extremely high.

- **Network effect.** The success of a currency depends on how many people use it and how well it's able to handle transactions. As more people adapt cryptocurrencies, it will speed up the pace of adaption and even more people will learn about them and adapt them. That's the beauty of network effects. If you get paid only in Bitcoins, companies that want you as a customer will be forced to accept your Bitcoins.

Hopefully after reading this, you've understood why exactly it's a gold mine right now. The next steps are to equip you with a shovel and teach you how to dig the gold, metaphorically speaking. Chapter 1 will teach you the fundamentals of the cryptocurrency technology like their origin, different options available in the market, how to store/trade cryptocurrencies etc. These are the basics. Without them, you won't experience much progress in further chapters. Chapter-2 deals with the Blockchain — the crux of the subject. You will learn what exactly mining is, what purpose it serves and why it is necessary. In chapters 3 & 5, you will learn what the roles and responsibilities of a miner are within the framework. Chapter-4 talks about the evolution of mining hardware and what you need to equip yourself with in order to be successful. Chapter 4 teaches you how to setup your own home mining rig using 8 GPUs. And the final chapter will help you understand where the cryptomining market is headed in the near future. So, it's a lot of useful knowledge and without further ado, let's get started.

Table of Contents

Why You Should Read This Book 10

Chatper-1: Overview of Cryptocurrency 15

Chatper-2: The Blockchain Ecosystem 51

Chatper-3: The Mining Process 84

Chatper-4: Mining Hardware and Software 94

Chatper-5: Mining Pools & Puzzles 107

Chatper-6: Installing your own Mining rig 113

Chatper-7: Future of Cryptocurrency Mining . 117

A few final words 129

More from the author 130

Chatper-1: Overview of Cryptocurrency

Before we dive into the nitty-gritty details of cryptocurrency mining, it is important to first understand exactly how they work. Terms like *blockchain*, *mining*, *cryptowallet* will appear frequently in later chapters. You will also need to be equipped with basic knowledge of cryptocurrency ecosystem before you can start dealing with various possible mining options. So, let's begin. We will start with the basics and slowly proceed to advanced concepts, tips and strategies.

The Origin of Cryptocurrency

Throughout history, we've used different mediums of exchange like commodity money, paper money, gold standard, fiat currencies etc. But over the years, different scientific communities across the world had been dissatisfied with the short-comings of these traditional currencies. Due to the explosion of internet and progress made in the fields of cryptography, online security, digital payments, it became possible to have a totally decentralized currency that could void the necessity of a central bank or government.

After the 9/11 attacks, America got very strict on the digital front. Laws like the *Patriot Act* were passed to perform online surveillance at a mass level. Needless to say, cryptocurrencies were shunned down owing to their decentralized structure and assumed to be hotbeds for terrorists and other illegal activities.

The first sign of cryptocurrency came when an American cryptographer named David Chaum founded the company *DigiCash* in Netherlands (since it was likely to get shut down in America). DigiCash used *blinding algorithms* to protect user's money and transaction details. However, they had complete monopoly over the supply of the currency and they dealt with the users directly. This made the Central Bank of

Netherlands call foul which meant that DigiCash would have to either sell the company or shut it down soon. Although Microsoft approached DigiCash with an offer of $180 million, Chaum thought that it was not enough. So, Microsoft took the offer off the table and DigiCash ran out of funds eventually.

Shortly after that, many cryptocurrency systems like *b-money* and *BitGold* came into light but never took off. They had all the necessary components like blockchain systems, anonymity protection, decentralization etc. but somehow couldn't get enough attention in the marketplace for widespread usage.

The first modern cryptocurrency to emerge that is effective and used widely is Bitcoin. A white-paper explaining the details of bitcoin implementation was first published under the pseudo-name of *Satoshi Nakamoto* in October 2008. The paper is titled *"Bitcoin: A Peer-to-Peer Electronic Cash System"* and can be downloaded at www.bitcoin.org/bitcoin.pdf. On January 2009, Satoshi released the initial version of the bitcoin software on SourceForge.net, opening the technology up to the public. To this day, the real identity of Satoshi Nakomoto remains a mystery. Based on bitcoin transaction logs, it is estimated that Satoshi owns roughly 1 million bitcoins which are currently evaluated at around 17 billion dollars!

Cryptocurrencies are slowly being accepted by all major companies and startups, especially in Silicon Valley. WordPress became the first major company to accept bitcoins in 2012. Soon after, big shots like Microsoft, Tesla, Dell, Virgin Group, Lamborghini followed. Currently, the total market cap for all cryptocurrencies has exceeded $630 billion. This is an indication that the world is slowly shifting towards decentralized cryptocurrencies for a myriad of reasons.

Different types of cryptocurrencies

More than 1000 public cryptocurrencies exist in the world and many more are created every month. In this section, we will look at the most prominent cryptocurrencies. To view the updated trends and market capitalizations of the top 100 cryptocurrencies, check out CoinMarketCap (www.coinmarketcap.com).

1. **Bitcoin (BTC):** This is the first known cryptocurrency that is well recognized and used by the public. It has paved the way for modern cryptocurrencies and is considered to be the de facto standard. Almost all the other cryptocurrencies have either branched off from or have major commonalities with bitcoin. Market cap of bitcoin stands at around 270 billion dollars by the end of 2017 making it the largest publicly traded digital currency. For a detailed guide on how Bitcoin works and how to properly invest in it, check out my book *"Bitcoin: The Digital Gold"* on Amazon.

2. **Litecoin (LTC)**: Launched around 2 years after bitcoin, litecoin is a decentralized peer-to-peer cryptocurrency with a growing network of developers, merchants and supporters. Although very similar to bitcoin, it offers relatively faster transaction confirmations. Where bitcoin is gold, litecoin is silver.

3. **Ethereum(ETH)**: Launched recently (2015), ethereum is also a decentralized cryptocurrency but offers more functionality like *smart contracts*, the *ethereum virtual machine*, distributed computing etc. As of Jan 2018, Ethereum is the second largest cryptocurrency with a market cap of around 100 billion dollars.

4. **Ripple (XRP)**: Ripple is heavily used by banks to settle global transactions in a secure and effective way at very low costs. It is different from bitcoin in its protocol and structure. Unlike bitcoin, ripple doesn't require high computing power for creation of new currency. As a result, it has a reduced network latency. The individual units of Ripple currency are called *ripples* (XRP). At the time of this writing, Ripple has a market capitalization of 48 billion dollars making it the third largest cryptocurrency.

5. **Dash (DASH)**: Originally known as DarkCoin, Dash is also a decentralized peer-to-peer cryptocurrency like Bitcoin albeit a more secretive one. It was launched in January 2014 and experienced a surge in traffic and fan-

following quickly. Its famous features include instant transactions (*InstantSend*) and complete private transactions (*PrivateSend*). It also uses a separate chained hashing algorithm called X11 unlike bitcoin's SHA256.

Note: Cryptocurrencies other than Bitcoin are referred to as "Altcoins" because they are alternatives launched after Bitcoin.

How to store cryptocurrencies

For regular fiat currencies, we all know where to store them i.e., in banks and wallets (online/offline). But how do you store cryptocurrencies? And how do you ensure that they're safe from thefts and attacks? We will look at how these problems are handled by a software called the "wallet" in the next section.

Cryptocurrency wallet

A cryptocurrency wallet, or *crypto-wallet* for short, is a digital holder for your cryptocurrency (like bitcoin) and is mandatory for performing transactions. It stores your private, public keys and manages your cryptocurrency transactions by interacting with the blockchain. There is no such thing as a bitcoin without a wallet identification. Every cryptocurrency unit has to be associated with, and transacted using, a wallet. You cannot spend your crypto-coins without the wallet. You also cannot spend the same crypto-coins from multiple wallets because it doesn't tally with the blockchain's record.

There are different types of wallets you can use like a desktop application, online wallet(website), hardware wallet (USB drive, hard disk etc.), paper wallet (printed sheet of keys in a QR code).

How does the wallet work?

A cryptowallet holds 3 primary values. The public key, private key and the amount of crypto-coins. As we've seen, the primary purpose of a wallet is to facilitate cryptocurrency transactions. Here's how it does it.

Let's say that you want to send bitcoins to your friend. Your wallet will generate the transaction-message, number of bitcoins you want to send and sign it with your private key and your friend's public key. This message is then communicated over an online network channel with your friend on it. Your friend's wallet will verify if the message is in fact sent by you and intended for him by decrypting it with his private key and your public key.

After the authenticity is established and the possibility of a middle-man is eliminated, your friend's wallet increases the number of bitcoins it holds and sends a response. Once your wallet receives the response, it decreases your bitcoin amount.

There is a specific Wallet protocol put in place to ensure that the amounts in the two wallets corresponding to a transaction are modified correctly. Anybody who wishes to implement their own wallet software must adhere to this protocol or else the transactions won't be processed.

After the amounts in both the wallets are modified, the blockchain is updated with the transaction entry. It takes some time for the blockchain network to validate the transaction. If all goes well, the ledger moves forward otherwise the error in the system will notify the wallets and the change is reverted. This concludes a typical wallet use-case scenario.

For the purpose of simplicity, many details have been omitted. If you're looking for more specifics, please visit the official bitcoin developer guide on this topic.

Security Measures for Wallets

Losing the wallet or the keys will result in ***TOTAL LOSS*** of your cryptocurrency. It might helpful to learn about a famous real-life story of James Howells who lost 7500 bitcoins (worth around $120 million today) because he accidentally threw his old hard drive into the trash bin while clearing his desk. That hard drive is now reportedly buried under four feet of junk in a landfill site in Newport. So, make no mistake, the security of your wallet should be your top most priority when dealing with cryptocurrency. Here are some tips to follow.

Tip #1: There are different wallet software you can choose for any cryptocurrency. Please use only an officially recognized wallet to avoid issues of security and malfunction. Take some time and go through the wallet specifications and your cryptocurrency's website to pick what's best. For bitcoin, you can find all the recommended bitcoin wallets at: www.bitcoin.org/en/choose-your-wallet.

Tip #2: Encrypt your wallet and private key and have multiple copies stored in secure locations (online and offline). Make sure that you have at least one copy available in an accessible physical device like a flash drive or a hard disk.

Tip #3: If the amount of your cryptocurrency is substantial, it is recommended to use multiple wallets to distribute the coins and reduce the possible damage that can happen. Use 2-step verification methods or MultiSig (Multiple Signature) transactions.

Cryptocurrency Exchanges

Also called *crypto-exchanges*, these are online platforms for buying and selling cryptocurrencies. You need to connect your wallet with a crypto-exchange to start trading or investing. You can also "buy-in" with your fiat currency after verifying your identity i.e. you can purchase BTC for, let's say, USD.

Just like regular company stocks can be traded at stock exchanges like NASDAQ, NYSE etc., cryptocurrencies can be traded at these crypto-exchanges. For a list of the top crypto exchanges, check out CryptoCoinCharts at the link below.
www.cryptocoincharts.info/markets/info

Please note that it's not necessary for an exchange to support all cryptocurrencies. And some of them might not be supported in your geographical area. So, browse through the exchanges carefully and select one that you find suitable. Here are some parameters to judge the exchange on: reputation and public opinion, supported payment options, transaction fee, geographical limitations, supported cryptocurrencies, ease of usage etc. (we will cover these shortly). The most popular exchanges are GDAX, Poloniex and Kraken.

I personally use GDAX/Coinbase (link below) because it satisfies all the essential criteria and offers a top-notch customer service. And so far, it has been a safe and smooth ride without any issue. It is also integrated with the Coinbase wallet so you don't need two separate accounts for managing both. I highly recommend it to beginners and anybody interested in cryptocurrency investing who wants a pleasant experience. Use the link below to sign up and get $10 bonus for your first trade.

www.bookstuff.in/coinbase

After picking a suitable exchange, you will need to verify your identity (via passport, driver's license etc.) to create an account. Once the account is created, you will be able to add/withdraw funds and start trading. Just like any other trading platform, you will be charged a very small fee for every trade to keep the exchange going.

You might be wondering as to why your ID is required when after all, cryptocurrencies are supposed to be decentralized and to support users' privacy/anonymity preferences. Well, here's the thing. Although the transactions themselves are private, the cryptocurrency exchange needs initial fiat currency to assign you crypto-coins to trade with. And where there is fiat currency involved, there is a non-zero probability of financial fraud. So, to avoid issues with unoriginal fiat currency (stolen credit cards etc.), the exchange does require your personal information to validate your fiat money. Once you've been verified, you can trade on the platform with privacy.

There are a few types of crypto exchanges that exist out there. So, it might help you to be aware of them before getting your feet wet.

1. **Traditional Crypto-Exchanges**: Similar to the old-school stock exchanges, these act as the "middle man" for traders looking to buy/sell

cryptocurrencies at market price. A slight fee is charged for every transaction to keep the exchange going. They also let users "buy in" with regular fiat currencies. Popular examples are: GDAX, Kraken, Shapeshift.

2. **Direct Trading Exchanges**: These are a kind of "unofficial" platforms where the trade doesn't happen at the fixed market price. Instead, sellers can set their own price and trade directly with buyers. Also referred to sometimes as peer-to-peer exchanges.

3. **Crypto Brokers**: These are independent platforms that offer cryptocurrency trading, customer support, development and other services. Similar to the currency exchange booths

at airports. Designed for a smooth trading experience, they provide trust and support to intermediate and advanced traders who find the traditional exchanges lacking in proper user interface and/or functionality. A good example for this is Coinbase.

Hey there! Just a quick break before we continue learning further. Let me ask you this – How do you feel? Are you already familiar with the concepts described here? Or are you enjoying learning about these new ideas and methods? Please let me know. I want you to write a review on Amazon by going to the link below. It will take no more than 2 minutes and would mean a lot to me. Thank you.

www.bookstuff.in/cryptomining-review

Now let's look at the factors to consider before selecting a cryptocurrency exchange. This is an important part of the buying process since you will be holding your crypto-coins on the exchange, sometimes for long periods of time. It's better to be safe than sorry. With that, let's dig into what exactly makes a good crypto-exchange and how to check if it suits your needs and preferences.

- **Credibility**: Do your research before selecting an exchange. When you find something that looks good, ask around and investigate a little. There are a lot of good forums that can assist you like BitcoinTalk (www.bitcointalk.org), CryptoCompare (www.cryptocompare.com), Reddit (www.reddit.com/r/CryptoMarkets) etc. You can also check out the latest Google News articles, Quora answers and do a general web search to get an idea of the exchange's trustworthiness.

- **Payment method**: Does the cryptoexchange accept your preferred method of payment? Are other options like PayPal, credit/debit cards, wire transfer also accepted in case you want to change your mode of payment? On a side note, cryptoexchanges usually charge an additional premium for credit cards due to the added risk and processing fee.

- **Identity Verification**: This is a sort of protection mechanism for the exchanges to prevent users from investing black money and other frauds. But always be careful when submitting your personal information to the exchange. Uploading a government-issued public ID like Driver's license or Passport should be fine.
- **Fees Structure**: This is something that changes with every cryptoexchange. You are usually charged for either deposit, withdrawal or transactions. Exchange rate is also something that influences your investments especially when done in large amounts. The exact percentages vary widely so you should always check the

cryptoexchange's website for complete details.

- **Geographical Restrictions**: This is again one of the factors that changes a lot between exchanges. You should check if the exchange offers *full* set of features and services in your country. Also, if you plan to do investing while on vacation in another country, you should check that as well.

Now that we are well versed in the basics like how cryptocurrencies are stored, how exchanges work, what to look at while picking an exchange etc., let's understand at a fundamental level, the answer to the following question.

Where do cryptocurrencies get value from?

One of the original reasons cryptocurrencies were invented is to store digital assets securely and avoid interference from central powers like the governments and banks. Some cryptocurrencies are backed by gold and precious metals while others have no backing except the widespread acceptance by users. So, if there is no backing from the governments and everything is distributed globally, where do cryptocurrencies actually get value from and what are the factors influencing it?

1. **Supply and Demand**: One of most popular economic principles is the correlation of price of an object with its supply & demand. Let's take Bitcoin for example. As we've already covered,

there can only be 21 million bitcoins in circulation due to the mining constraints. There are 7 billion people on this planet and as the adoption of Bitcoin as a global currency grows, there will be friction in the market caused due to growing demand and increasingly limited supply. This friction will lead to the rise in value of Bitcoin. It will also be amplified due to the fact that the popular strategy among many crypto-investors seems to be to "buy and hold".

2. **Mining difficulty**: Unlike fiat currencies which are minted by the national governments based on various monetary policies, cryptocurrencies are mined by volunteers. Mining cryptocurrencies requires a lot of electrical and processing power. And the cost is not getting any cheaper. So, the

inherent difficulty involved in creating a unit of cryptocurrency leads to a certain perceived value. This goes up as the mining difficulty increases. Basic economics states that the price of something that is rare and valuable will be high. Many cryptocurrencies use POW (Proof of Work) protocol while mining new coins and validating transactions. And the POW protocol rewards miners who have spent more time and effort solving harder problems. This is a fair way to incentivize the miners and also ensure that there is a direct correlation between the price of the cryptocurrency and mining difficulty. For more details on this, check out my book *"Blockchain: The Technology Revolution behind Bitcoin and Cryptocurrency"* on Amazon.

3. **User Requirements**: If a cryptocurrency has no practical benefits to users, how is it any good? The cryptocurrency has to solve user's problems to be considered valuable. This is similar to how a company's stock value will plummet if it's not delivering any good quality products/services to its customers. In addition to being a means of value exchange, many cryptocurrencies offer distinctive solutions to domains like legal contracts, digital security, Internet of Things etc. This makes the investors fund the project and the customers register and use it.

4. **Public Opinion**: This is one of the most underrated causes of price surges for not only cryptocurrencies but any other publicly traded stock/commodity. Despite what we may believe,

a majority of people think emotionally and take decisions based on their gut. The term "panic selling" is famous among traders and investors. Any major news like a security breach or a market crisis will make the value drop. This happened in Feb 2014 when Mt.Gox, the most famous crypto-exchange at that time filed for bankruptcy as a result of cyber-attacks. When it comes to Bitcoin, a lot of people believe that the independent decentralized nature of currency will be more beneficial since it is less prone to corruption, fraud and manipulation by central banks and governments. The other side of the coin (no pun intended) is that there are also a lot of people who believe that Bitcoin is a currency used mostly by drug-dealers and criminals online. Nevertheless, the fact of the matter is that cryptocurrencies are blowing up globally and more people are becoming aware of the current crypto landscape and what it has to offer.

5. **Media & Law:** The price of a cryptocurrency can rise or fall depending on how the media portrays it to the public. There is always the possibility of getting blindsided by manipulative media. A few corporations or individuals who hold vested interest in a cryptocurrency can publicize its ICO (Initial Coin Offering) to bloat up its price in the market. This is why you should always do proper market research and look into a wide variety of sources including reddit forums, quora answers, facebook groups, google news/trends and multiple news and publishing articles. If you're tech-savvy, I would also advise

you to delve into the source code and developer updates. Legal notices, Nation-wide bans and anti-cryptocurrency policies have also been observed in the recent past. Countries like China, Vietnam and Russia are active in their protest against public usage of bitcoin. This caused a temporary dip in the price of bitcoin but soon bounced back up to an all-time high. Meanwhile, many countries like Canada, UK, Australia are embracing the crypto-revolution and have provided infrastructure and policy support to the cryptocurrency communities. Some of them even have Bitcoin ATMs available across various cities.

6. **Investors**: The fact that a cryptocurrency startup has received funding from a good investor can boost its coin price in the market.

Investments are generally considered signs of trust. So, when a good/popular investor decides to put in capital for growing a cryptocurrency, a large portion of people decide to place their bets on it as well. Some malicious investors can also try to buy a large portion of the coins, inflate the price with press-releases or promotions and then sell them off quickly without any real progress. This is also referred to as the *pump and dump* strategy. The investors thus have a considerably high impact on the pricing of cryptocurrencies (especially altcoins with lower market caps).

7. **Market dilution**: With more than 1000 cryptocurrencies currently in the market and more coming in every year, the market sure has gotten crowded with so many alternatives. Even

if an innovative solution is offered by a brand-new cryptocurrency in the market, it doesn't take too long before a competitor opens shop with lesser token price and upgraded capabilities. This causes frequent and unexpected spikes in the prices of cryptocurrencies. Bitcoin, though, is considered a reserve cryptocurrency since it has the highest market cap and largest user-base, owing to its first mover advantage. Fluctuation in bitcoin price usually causes a ripple effect and creates a fluctuation in prices of other cryptocurrencies as

Chatper-2: The Blockchain Ecosystem

In this chapter, we will look at the foundation on which most cryptocurrencies rely on – the blockchain. If you're a beginner to this technology, make sure to take your time while going through the different sections. It is going to get a bit technical. Reference links have been provided where necessary for better understanding.

What is Blockchain?

Let us begin by asking the question – what do we need a currency for? We need currency so that we can give it to others (buying) or take it from others (selling). Isn't this true? And for a cryptocurrency, that is where a blockchain comes into the picture. Blockchain is a technology that allows people to transfer cryptocurrency between one another securely. It is a distributed database where all the transaction records are saved. Unlike a typical fiat currency like USD, the blockchain of cryptocurrency is distributed and spread across various countries and individuals. The databases and servers are run by volunteers who maintain a peer-to-peer network. There is no possibility of government or any third-party involvement in manipulating the database records. Even if the government officials or any malicious entities volunteer for maintaining the blockchain, they cannot alter the transaction records due to the constraints imposed by its design.

Blockchain is essentially an open electronic ledger where all transactions are recorded for public viewing. These transactions are grouped together into blocks for optimization purposes i.e., it is faster to verify blocks of transactions than individual transactions. And as the name suggests, the blockchain is essentially a chain of valid blocks connected together. All the latest bitcoin transactions can be found at: www.blockchain.info. This open strategy of blockchain prevents counterfeits and other frauds. By checking the blockchain, you can be sure that the transactions are completely legitimate. Once you make a transaction, it will appear shortly in the public blockchain.

You might be wondering, *"But won't people know who's spending how much by looking at the blockchain?"*. The answer to that is *No* because your identity is protected using encryption and mapping functions. Only your Wallet-ID will appear in the blockchain which reveals nothing about your personal identity. We will cover the mechanics of a cryptocurrency wallet in the next chapter.

What is Mining?

Now that we have an idea of what the blockchain is, it is necessary to understand how it is updated unanimously throughout the network. It has to be unanimous because if the status of blockchain is not congruent among the nodes, it will lead to discrepancies in verifying transactions which will result in frauds and eventual system failure. So, let's look into this in detail.

There are two kinds of nodes in a blockchain network. Normal nodes and mining nodes. Both of these have their own separate operating protocols. And every node maintains its own blockchain, constructed individually by adding valid blocks to the list. The normal nodes have relatively basic functionality. They receive transaction-messages from neighboring nodes in the network and their job is to verify the transactions and propagate them forward to remaining nodes. This will ensure that as time goes by, only verified transactions are spread across the network. This is a basic layer of security to ensure bogus transactions are not updated in the blockchain.

Now, the mining nodes are a different kind of nodes that execute the *mining protocol* which includes the following steps.

→ Listen for new transactions and verify them.

→ Aggregate verified transactions into a block.

→ Compute the solution to an algorithm called *Proof-of-Work* for that specific block.

→ Timestamp the block along with the computed *proof-of-work solution* and broadcast it across the network.

The mining nodes essentially group new valid transactions into blocks and propagate them to other nodes. The validity of the block can be measured by any node by checking the *proof-of-work* value. So, when this new block is received by the remaining nodes, they check its validity and add it to their own blockchain. A reward is given to the mining node that propagated the valid block with the earliest timestamp. This reward is usually a certain amount of cryptocurrency units. It is similar to the processing fee charged by banks and other financial organizations. Once a block is verified and added to the blockchain, it is said to have been successfully mined.

Now we know how blocks are mined, how the blockchain is built and how the *Proof-of-Work* protocol helps in making sure that every node on the network is on the same page when it comes to the blockchain. Here's the interesting part. In most cryptocurrencies (including Bitcoin), mining is the only way to create new crypto-coins. That is to say, the only way for the system to assign value to the cryptocurrency is to measure the amount of computation performed by the mining nodes. Every bitcoin ever mined has been the result of a mining node performing the *Proof-of-Work* algorithm to create a new valid block.

So, the purpose of mining is twofold. To create new cryptocurrency and update the blockchain with valid transactions. The reason that miners are rewarded is to incentivize them to perform the needed computation. If there was no reward, there wouldn't be enough miners to validate the transactions quickly. This would lead to high latency in the network which would make the whole system rather unsafe. The security of the cryptocurrency depends on how fast the transactions are verified. And that depends on how many miners are competing for the reward simultaneously. This is the beauty of the bitcoin-blockchain system design. And also, the reward for mining goes down by 50% every 4 years for the bitcoin system. Eventually, there would be no reward for mining blocks except for the transaction fee and tips. This is a way to limit the supply of the cryptocurrency and ensure its value doesn't go down below a certain threshold.

The Blockchain is the heart of most cryptocurrencies. It is the bedrock on which all the transactions, security and efficiency of the system rely upon. Moreover, the tech community across the globe is waking up to the ingenuity of the blockchain design. Numerous applications of the blockchain technology are being identified in all areas of the digital spectrum. It may as well be that we've stumbled upon the backbone of a new kind of internet. If you're really interested in learning more about this to get a complete perspective, check out my book *"Blockchain: The Technology Revolution behind Bitcoin and Cryptocurrency"* on Amazon.

The two main problems that a blockchain solves are:

1. Decentralized Consensus
2. Double Spending

How Decentralized Consensus Works

The architecture of the blockchain is such that it eliminates the need for a central database or monitoring authority. You have to understand that this is a groundbreaking technological revolution not only in the field of digital currency but also in business, banking, governance, politics etc. A plethora of possibilities have opened up after it has been proven that a system like bitcoin can be developed which achieves decentralized consensus in a secure and efficient manner. New self-verifying systems and decentralized apps are being developed today on account of this innovation.

To those who are unaware, decentralized consensus is a scenario where a network of entities comes to a common agreement about something (in our case, the validity of a transaction) without having to trust one another. This is also known as distributed trust-less consensus and is a major research topic in the field of Distributed Systems. Many algorithms have been designed to solve this problem of distributed consensus. Cryptocurrencies like Bitcoin use a specific protocol called *Proof of Work* (POW), as we've seen, which lets the blockchain network achieve distributed consensus and operate without getting tampered with. It is important to understand why achieving distributed consensus is so important in a cryptocurrency's blockchain network.

Let's assume that you have a network of computers (or "nodes") that are interconnected in a haphazard manner. This network forms the *backend* of your service. In other words, all the computation and database storage operations are handled by this network *behind the scenes*. Your objective is to ensure that when a user performs an action, it has to be recorded and updated congruently throughout the network. So, your network is distributed but you have to project a single consistent experience to users everywhere. This is the most basic requirement for not only a cryptocurrency like bitcoin but also for almost every technology company out there like Google, Facebook, Amazon, Instagram etc.

When a user performs an action, you will observe that in order to achieve the objective of consistency, you are inevitably left with only two options. Either record this action in all the nodes or none of the nodes. If you record it in only some of the nodes, there is an inconsistency in the network and the nodes cannot figure out the truth i.e., whether the user did actually perform the action or not. In other words, the network cannot come to an agreeable consensus. This is a big problem because an inconsistent network is an insecure network. Any hacker would be able to exploit this inconsistency to spread viruses or manipulate the database to his/her advantage. Therefore, it is important for a distributed network to maintain consistent data across all nodes and be able to identify erroneous and inconsistent records quickly. This is the reason why distributed consensus is so important in a blockchain network.

Now let's look at how exactly the blockchain aids in achieving this decentralized consensus. We will be considering bitcoin as the reference cryptocurrency.

Decentralized consensus in a blockchain is truly amazing. This is because all the nodes in the network are able to agree on the validity of a transaction without having to trust anyone else or knowing the identity of parties involved. That is why it is also known as trust-less decentralized consensus.

Decentralized consensus in a cryptocurrency using blockchain is achieved in an emergent manner. What this means is that there is no single point of time at which all the nodes in the network are able to agree on the validity of a transaction. As time progresses, more and more nodes will be able to arrive at the same conclusion.

There are four phases in which this emergent distributed consensus is achieved. Let's look at them closely.

Phase #1: Verification of every incoming transaction by every node.

The nodes in the network receive data regarding various transactions from their neighboring nodes. Some of these transactions are just invalid. So, as a primary rule, all the nodes check the incoming transactions and collect the valid ones into what is called as a *transaction pool* or *mempool*. The transactions are verified using cryptographic techniques based on a list of criteria that are public.

And this pool of valid but unconfirmed transactions are propagated across the network by each node. So, all the invalid transactions are weeded out by the nodes in the network in the first phase.

Phase #2: Mining nodes accumulate valid transactions into blocks.

Mining nodes, as we've seen earlier, are special nodes in the network whose job is to collect valid transactions from their neighboring nodes, put them in a block and compute a unique value ("*Proof of Work*") for the block using a cryptographic algorithm. The mining nodes keep track of the latest blocks and compete with each other to create a new block of these valid transactions with the appropriate *proof-of-work*.

These blocks are then propagated across the network to other nodes.

Phase #3: Nodes receive and verify blocks

As the nodes in the network receive blocks from various mining nodes, they calculate their validity. Anybody can accumulate transactions into blocks. But the trick here is that computing the correct *"proof-of-work"* of a block is very hard and therefore reduces the chance of a transaction fraud. Once the nodes receive a mining node's block, they verify it against the *"proof-of-work"* and add it to their blockchain which they've been maintaining and updating so far.

Phase #4: Nodes eliminate irrelevant blocks

Every node maintains and updates its own blockchain which is essentially a list of blocks that are considered valid using publicly known and accepted criteria. Nodes can receive multiple valid blocks by different mining nodes. So how can they decide collectively as to which of the received blocks should be considered while extending the blockchain? This is where the proof-of-work protocol comes in handy. Different blocks have different proof-of-work values. The bitcoin protocol states that while selecting blocks, preference should be given to the block with the highest proof-of-work value. So, if a node gets two different blocks, it will maintain two separate lists in the blockchain until one of them exceeds the other in the total cumulative proof-of-work value sum. It will then discard the sub-chain with lower proof-of-work value sum. In a way, the nodes give preference to the sub-chain in which the mining nodes have spent more computational power because the *proof-of-work* value sum is a measure of the amount of computation done by the mining nodes.

The Double-Spending Problem

The concept of blockchain was first brought to light by the Bitcoin inventor, Satoshi Nakamoto. It was (and still is) considered a brilliant engineering design partly because it was able to solve what no other digital currency could before that point of time which is to *'Ensure that the cryptocurrency units cannot be spent more than once.'* This is termed as the double spending problem.

Unlike fiat currency, the problem with a virtual currency is not the creation of the currency units. Anybody can come up with protocols/algorithms defining how the virtual currency units need to be created, how they need to be structured, what the size (in bytes) of each unit should be and so on. But the fundamental problem that any currency, especially a digital currency, needs to solve is *Double Spending*.

A *double-spend* is a scenario in which one unit of currency is spent in two separate transactions. This can be done by duplicating the unit itself or manipulating the record of transactions. In case of cryptocurrencies, this 'record' is the blockchain ledger.

A typical fiat currency solves the double-spending problem by deploying special techniques to print the cash and identify fake bills. The banks that deal with fiat currency transactions also take extensive security measures to prevent their databases (which hold all the transaction and account details) from getting hacked and hijacked. If the security of the bank's computer-network was compromised, the potential for damage is huge. With countless cases of bank frauds, hacking attacks and duplication of cash, it is evident that a fiat currency's solution to the double-spending problem is undoubtedly flawed.

So, how does a cryptocurrency like bitcoin solve this?

Unlike a centralized fiat currency, a system like bitcoin does not maintain "balances" of the individuals. It only maintains a ledger of transactions a.k.a the blockchain. So, the only way to handle this issue is by assigning identifiers to bitcoins so that when someone tries to spend a bitcoin with the same identifier twice, it can be checked against the transactions recorded in the blockchain.

The way this works is, whenever you send someone bitcoins, that transaction is identified and recorded using a UTXO which is short for Unspent Transaction Output. This UTXO is the unique identifier that represents a transaction of bitcoins which is similar to a bill of fiat currency. UTXOs can be spent only as wholes. But they can be converted into multiple smaller UTXOs for transaction convenience.

When you want to spend some bitcoins, you have to either merge or split two UTXOs to create the new set of UTXOs you want. For example, assume that you have two UTXOs of 0.3 and 0.6 bitcoins, received from Alice and Bob respectively. Let's refer to these using their IDs, X and Y. So, X represents the UTXO of Alice and Y that of Bob.

And let's say that you want to send 0.7 bitcoins to Carter. The conversion goes as follows:

X (0.3 bitcoins) + Y (0.6 bitcoins) =>
Z (0.7 bitcoins) + W (0.2 bitcoins)

Z and W represent the unique IDs of two new UTXOs created so that 0.7 bitcoins can be sent to Carter. Now, this new UTXO (Z) can only be spent when used in conjunction with Carter's signature. It is propagated across the network and eventually picked up by a mining node which hashes it into a block and updates the blockchain. That is how the transaction takes place. And the conversion is handled by a software called the *cryptocurrency wallet* which we'll be looking into in the next chapter. The other UTXO (W) worth

0.2 bitcoins goes back into your wallet and is spendable only in conjunction with your signature.

With this framework in place, all that a node has to do to verify if a bitcoin is being "double-spent" is to check the UTXO ID against the blockchain's transactions. Even if a node's blockchain is incomplete, the faulty UTXO will get propagated only so far before getting dropped by the other nodes with complete blockchain which can verify latest transactions.

Who maintains the servers and Why?

You must be wondering, if maintaining and updating the blockchain takes so much effort, who would want to do this? Why would anyone want to volunteer for this kind of a task?

The answer to that is *Mining incentives.* As we've already seen, most cryptocurrencies are designed in such a way that the people who validate transactions and update the blockchain are rewarded with new crypto-coins. This serves as an incentive for their efforts. Rewarding the miners is the only sustainable way of maintaining a distributed decentralized cryptocurrency network. This is because mining the crypto-coins requires a lot of computational power provided by specialized GPUs and also involves paying a lot of money in electricity bill.

It also happens to be that mining is the only way of generating cryptocurrency i.e., the new crypto-coins in the network are only generated when a miner creates a new valid block. This is a clever strategy to solve two problems in one shot. The miners get incentivized and the network gets new crypto-coins to work with.

It is very important for the system to be designed in such a way that **anybody** can come in and volunteer as a miner in the network. If the ability to mine was exclusive, the banks or the government or the top 1% could find a way to attain too much control over the system. This could jeopardize the safety and decentralization of the cryptocurrency. For example, if a bank was bombed and/or it's servers were hacked, it's customers would be in trouble. But with a widespread network of mining volunteers, there wouldn't be a single point of failure. This was something that Satoshi Nakomoto made sure of, while designing the system framework.

Why is it safe?

For the purpose of answering this question, let's narrow our focus down to one single cryptocurrency – bitcoin. Bitcoin is the most widely used cryptocurrency in the world. Millions of people pay close attention to the bitcoin network every day. The software itself undergoes regular public updates. A 2013 article on Forbes suggests that the global bitcoin computing power is 256 times more than the top 500 supercomputers in the world. That should give you a measure of the number of servers being run by the bitcoin volunteers. So, at this point of time, the only possible ways to hack bitcoin are either taking down the internet or cracking the SHA256 function. SHA256 is one of the most famous security functions used in the Bitcoin protocol to encrypt data into output of 256-bits (32 bytes) size. It is deemed to be uncrackable. This of course, is regarding the overall bitcoin network and the system design. You can still get your bitcoins lost/stolen if you do not follow the recommended security measures (described in the next chapter) while operating your wallet.

Although cracking the SHA256 algorithm is next to impossible, it is important to understand the difference between safety and anonymity in the context of cryptocurrencies. The fact that SHA256 is hard to crack only implies that an attack on the blockchain or stealing your crypto-coins is extremely unlikely. It, however, does not mean that you are anonymous within the system. This is one of the biggest misconceptions about bitcoin and other cryptocurrencies. Your bitcoins are safe but your identity is not a total secret.

Most cryptocurrencies including Bitcoin only provide pseudonymity and not complete anonymity. Although your identity is not revealed openly, the transaction details are updated on the blockchain which is accessible by anyone.

Using techniques like cluster analysis and pattern recognition on the data from the public blockchain, one can start to form associations with your activity and your IP-address (which is essentially your online identity). Now, you can use software like Tor or VPN to hide your IP address but the fact of the matter is that even Tor cannot guarantee complete anonymity. A dedicated hacker with enough resources can eventually track your IP address down. But, he/she will not be able to steal or tamper with your crypto-coins as long as you follow the proper security measures and store your crypto-coins in a safe wallet. Having said that, if you're still concerned, I would recommend that you choose Zcash as it is the most pseudonymous cryptocurrency out there.

Chatper-3: The Mining Process

Now that we know how the blockchain works and what cryptomining is, let's look at this from the perspective of a miner. How do you become a miner? What tasks do you do as a miner? And how does this whole business operate? We will be looking at these questions and more in the upcoming sections. The prerequisite for this is to join the appropriate cryptocurrency network and be connected to the other nodes. Once this is setup, there are six essentials tasks you need to perform as a miner:

1. **Listen for transactions:** This is the most basic function of a mining node. It has to read the transactions passing through the

network and validate them by checking the signatures and UTXOs.

2. **Maintain a private blockchain:** When a new node joins the mining network, it will prepare its own blockchain by fetching existing data from neighboring nodes. After that, it has to listen to the network for broadcasts about new blocks and validate them. If the transactions within the block are valid and if the block's nonce is also valid, it will be added to the blockchain and propagated.

3. **Create a new block:** After you keep listening for new blocks and updating your private blockchain, you'll end up at a point where your private blockchain is up-to-date with the public blockchain. This is when you can

try to go ahead of the curve and start forming new blocks to update the blockchain. You'll need to grab all latest "unrecorded" transactions, validate them and put them into a new block that is the extension of the last known valid block.

4. **Solve POW and find a nonce:** Once all the elements of the block are formed, you need to find a nonce that makes it valid. This requires a lot of computation and time because you need to solve the *Proof of Work* algorithm for the new block.

5. **Propagate the block:** Once you calculate the proper nonce, you are tentatively in possession of a valid block which can potentially become an update to the public blockchain. The only thing left is to beat the

other miners to it. So, you'll have to timestamp your block, sign it and send it to neighboring nodes. If you're lucky, the block will be accepted and the buck moves forward.

6. **Get rewarded:** If your block was accepted by the other nodes and updated to the public blockchain, you will be sent the mining prize + transaction fees to your wallet address.

If you look at these tasks a bit closely, you'll notice that validation is only part of the equation. As a miner, competition plays a major role in deciding your effectiveness. Unless you're quick to propagate a valid block, all the time and effort that went into validating the block becomes useless. The cryptocurrency network feeds off of this competition because it leads to faster transaction processing and lower latency.

Now, let's look at the most important step in the mining process that will help you leave the competition behind if you do it right.

Finding a valid nonce

To recap from chapter-2, every block contains a variable parameter called the "nonce" (number used only once) that will change the hash output. The goal of the miner is to find a nonce such that the hash output of the block has a target number of zeroes in the beginning.

Every block contains a header and the transactions. The header contains the block's metadata such as the pointer to the previous block, the nonce, hash output etc. The transactions are contained in a structure called the "merkle tree". Think of it as a family-tree sort of structure with a parent node linked to its 2 children each of which will in turn be linked to 2 of their own children and so on.

Here's an image of the block structure with the merkle tree depiction.

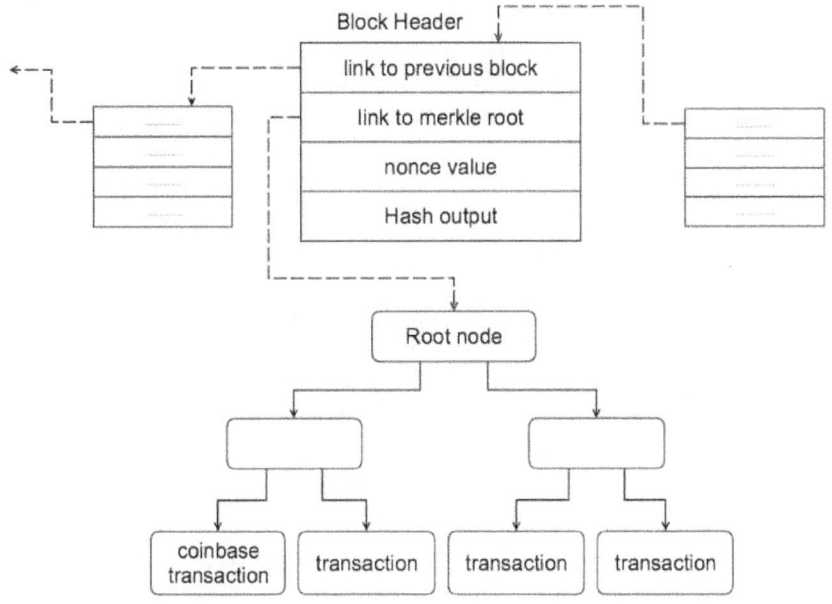

All the transactions in a block are represented in this merkle tree structure. The top-most node is the root of the merkle tree. From this root, you can access any node of the merkle tree by following the appropriate links to the children. Anyways, the bottom line is that the root of the merkle tree is all you need to access a block's transactions. And this root node is present in the block's header as well.

So, as a miner, your responsibility is to take all the new transactions and compile them into a merkle tree. During this process, keep in mind that the limit of the block size cannot be exceeded. Once your merkle tree is built, add a pointer to its root node to the block header. Now, all you have to do is find a nonce value in the header that meets the target. So, you start iterating all values of nonce from zero and check if you can find something that fits. The nonce-field has 32 bits in the header. Therefore, you will have to iterate over 2 raised to 32 possibilities at the most.

But here's the catch. Many times, you will exhaust all possibilities of the nonce in the header before finding a solution. Does this mean your block is un-mineable? Well, not exactly. You see, there is another parameter whose value you change to meet the target. This parameter is called the "coinbase transaction" parameter and it is present in the merkle tree. It is also called the "generation transaction" and has nothing to do with the Coinbase wallet platform we discussed in Chapter-3.

The coinbase transaction is essentially the first transaction in a block and includes a special field that can take upto 100 bytes of arbitrary input from the miner. So, if you've exhausted all possibilities of the header-nonce, you can iterate over this coinbase field to find a solution. Keep in mind that the coinbase transaction is a part of the merkle tree. So, if you change its value, the merkle tree changes which means the root node will change. Therefore, you will have to update the new root node in the block's header before proceeding.

Chatper-4: Mining Hardware and Software

Today, cryptomining has gotten so big that the world's biggest chip manufacturer, TSMC, has reported substantial profits from delivering mining related hardware. More and more miners are demanding efficient hardware and software solutions to stay ahead of competition. In this chapter, we will look at the state of the market in terms of the hardware and software requirements to be a successful cryptominer.

Mining Hardware

If you have an AMD Radeon 5800 (or newer) graphics card with your computer, you can install an appropriate mining software, join a mining pool and get started with mining. However, as more and more volunteers join the miner community, it is becoming increasingly clear that you have to know your hardware if you want to survive the race to mine all the coins. So, we will look at various possible hardware setups that allow us to mine cryptocurrencies and how they've been modified for efficiency over the years.

CPU Mining

This was the first phase in the evolution of cryptomining. People used the CPU (Central Processing Unit) chips from their computers for solving the mining puzzles. The SHA256 hashes were computed in a linear fashion on their PCs and Macs in an attempt to find a valid nonce. The software for this computation literally had less than 10 lines of code. But since it was run on a general-purpose computer, it was not very well optimized. But they're still able to compute nearly 20 million hashes per second. Today, CPU Mining is considered one of the worst possible ways of cryptocurrency mining and anyone who attempts it is presumed to be delusional.

GPU Mining

GPU stands for Graphical Processing Unit. These are graphic cards that go alongside CPUs and provide support in displaying all kinds of visual stuff you see on your computer monitor. It so happens that handling graphics requires a high degree of parallel computing and quick execution. So, GPUs are a much better fit for CryptoMining than CPUs because you can compute multiple hashes at the same time and find a valid nonce quicker.

In the past, GPU mining for Bitcoin was a profitable prospect because GPUs are not too expensive, they can be setup easily and they can be programmed using a language called OpenCL. You can use GPU to calculate upto 200 million hashes per second which is higher throughput than CPUs but still not sufficient for present day mining (for bitcoin).

Advantages of GPU Mining:

1. **Overclocking.** This is a feature that allows the device to run faster than what it's designed for but at the risk of running into some errors. This a desirable feature in gaming because you don't mind if a few pixels are off as long as the core is correct. And with mining as well, if your advantage of speed outweighs the disadvantage of error, overclocking will turn out to be profitable.
2. **Bitwise operations.** GPUs have certain instructions hardcoded in them that allow for a faster computation of SHA256 outputs.
3. **Scalability.** You can run multiple GPUs from one single CPU and motherboard. So, you

can stack them up in one place as long as they're kept cool enough.

<u>Disadvantages of GPU Mining:</u>

1. A lot of electronic circuitry inside a GPU is irrelevant for mining. Some of this circuitry is used for performing "floating point" operations which have no use when it comes to calculating SHA256 hashes.
2. They heat up rather quickly if you stack them up and place them in an enclosed environment without proper ventilation/cooling. Typically, graphics cards were designed for solo-use for a single computer to aid in rendering better, faster visuals. So, this thermal factor wasn't

considered while designing the GPU hardware.

3. *"With great power comes great processing."* But also comes a great electricity bill. GPUs consume a substantial amount of charge to run efficiently and thus will cost you a lot. An average Nvidia GeForce graphic card has a power wattage of more than 1000.

FPGA Mining

FPGA is short for *Field Programmable Gate Array*. They are Integrated Circuits that can be programmed based on the need as opposed to other hardware chips which can only perform one type of operation after manufacture. FPGAs have all the advantages of GPUs and none of the disadvantages. They are also a lot faster and smaller in size. A proper FPGA setup can get you upto 1 billion hashes per second. Amazed by this speed? Don't be. With this rate, it would take you more than a lifetime to find a valid Bitcoin block even with 100 FPGA boards. But FPGAs were a crucial stepping stone in the process of figuring out the best possible mining hardware. Here is an image of an FPGA module (source: Wikipedia).

ASIC Mining

This is the latest and most effective solution we have today when it comes to Cryptomining. ASIC stands for *Application Specific Integrated Circuits*. They are special breed of chips specifically designed for mining cryptocurrency like Bitcoin. It takes a lot of careful effort to develop a proper Bitcoin ASIC. However, in a rush to mine Bitcoins, the industry has produced these in a surprisingly little time. The hash rate of the Bitcoin network keeps getting updated. So, to catch up to this wave, there was a lot of pressure on ASIC sellers to deliver the chips as soon as possible. The goal was to get the chip at the earliest and start mining before the difficulty and the network hash rate catch up.

Mining Software

In this section, we will look at 3 possible software suites you can use to actually get started with mining on your own hardware. For bitcoin specifically, you can get a full list of compatible mining software at the following link: https://bitcoin.it/wiki/Mining_software

CGMiner

This is one of the best programs available for beginners. Compatible with almost all operating systems (including Windows, Mac and Linux), it uses a simple CLI (Command Line Interface) to receive user command and execute on them. After installation, you will be prompted to enter the credentials of the mining pool you want to join. All connected devices available for mining will be automatically detected and listed. The CGMiner software is written in C programming language and is an open source project. It provides features like Hardware Monitoring, Overclocking, Remote Interface, Fan control.

BitMinter

The BitMinter software has a friendly GUI (Graphical User Interface) and comes with preinstalled mining pool settings. Unfortunately, these settings are fixed only for the Bitminter pool which is actually one of the longest running and credible pools in the market. So, the BitMinter client you run on your computer will directly connect with their pool and show you all kinds of stats for your hardware's performance. Most notably, you can check your harsh rate, time spent and success rate. For more details on their reward policy and server locations, check out their website at www.bitminter.com.

MultiMiner

This is a friendlier version of BFGMiner that works well with ASIC and FGPA hardware but not so much with GPUs. With useful features combined with graphical interface, it is a delight for mining newbies. As with CGMiner, you will be prompted to enter the pool information after installation and your hardware will be automatically detected and scanned for mining potential. You can look up data on different pools, average hash power, projected daily profit etc. One of the most useful features that this program provides is an option to automatically choose the most profitable coin to mine with your hardware.

Chatper-5: Mining Pools & Puzzles

Historically, solo miners have had to face a lot of trouble making profits in this business because the mining difficulty keeps rising because of the competition and reward keeps diminishing because of the mining protocol. To counter this effect, people have come up with the idea of creating mining pools where miners share their resources to find valid blocks and distribute the rewards between themselves appropriately. This is similar to insurance or mutual funds for crypto miners.

Mining Pools

In a mining pool, all the miners try to mine the next valid block. The *recipient* field in the block is filled with a pre-selected address. This address belongs to the *pool manager* who will distribute the reward among the miners after receiving it. This distribution is done based on the work done by the individual miners. Also, the pool manager will take a cut of the reward as commission.

Now, how does the pool manager decide how much work was done by an individual miner? In chapter-2, we've learnt that a valid block has to have a certain number of zeroes in the beginning of its hash. This number is called the target. Let's suppose that the target is 50. So only blocks that have 50 or more zeroes in the beginning of their hash are considered valid. And the first node to find such a block gets the reward obviously. But miners in a mining pool submit blocks called as *shares*. These are blocks that are almost valid but they have slightly fewer zeroes than the target in their hash. The more *shares* a miner is able to produce, the more work he has done in the mining pool and the more his reward.

This is how a mining pool works. Some may think that it's unfair because even if you find a valid block, you will only be rewarded proportional to the amount of work you've done i.e., the number of shares you were able to produce. As such, many miners hop/switch pools to maximize their rewards. Research is currently going on as to what an optimal reward system of a mining pool should be. Nevertheless, mining pools are great opportunities for small/solo miners to grab a piece of the pie in exchange for their contribution.

Mining Puzzles

These are the problems that miners have to solve in order to find a valid block and get rewarded. Since a personal incentive is attached to solving mining puzzles, the system adapts itself so that profits are maximized. However, there may be some necessary work that may get left out because of this. So, it is important to design the mining puzzle in such a way that rewards are given out for doing the most essential work.

Otherwise, the work wouldn't be done. That's just what the laws of economics and human psychology dictate. Let us look at the 3 crucial characteristics that a mining puzzle should possess.

1. **Quick Verification**: The puzzle can be hard to solve but it should be quick to verify because that will help in faster update of the blockchain which will result in faster transactions and better security.
2. **Adjustable Difficulty**: Of course, the puzzle can be designed to have a parameter that changes the difficulty of solving it. And this is key because if the difficulty was fixed, the mining rate would change with the hash power available in the network. Having

adjustable difficulty lets us streamline the process of mining and keep a constant interval for finding valid blocks.

3. **Progress Freeness:** A fair mining puzzle will distribute the power and let anyone find the solution. The probability of finding the solution should be proportional to the amount of hash power you can contribute. This characteristic of puzzle where solving it is independent of the amount of work you've already put in is called Progress freeness.

The mining puzzle for Bitcoin is known as SHA256 partial preimage. And it satisfies all the 3 criteria discussed previously.

Chatper-6: Installing your own Mining rig

As we've seen previously, mining Bitcoin with GPUs is no longer profitable but you can still use them for other cryptocurrencies like Ethereum, ZCash etc. So, let's look at the process for setting up your own home cryptomining rig.

The first question you need to ask before beginning is: what hardware do I want to use? The GPUs are the crux of the mining rig so you have to select them carefully. The most famous options available in the market are Nvidia and AMD. Both of them are quite suitable for mining in 2018 and beyond. However, in this book, we will be taking Nvidia as the example.

Listed below is all the hardware you'll need to setup the rig. The motherboard can support upto 8 GPUs so we want to take full advantage of this capability.

Recommended Hardware

Motherboard: ASUS PRIME Z270-A LGA1151

Processor: Intel Celeron G3930 BX80677G3930

RAM: Ballistix Sport - BLS16G4D26BFSC 288 pin

Power supply Unit: EVGA SuperNOVA 1000W

GPU: GIGABYTE GeForce GTX 1060 (6 of these)

SSD Storage: Silicon Power 32GB SATA III

PCI-E Risers: Graphics Extension Cable 1X to 16X

The Geforce GTX1060 offers 80% hash rate(22MH/s) of GTX1070 at only 50% of the cost. It also consumes lesser power than 1070. So it is considered to be a better option especially for beginners.

Here are the configuration steps for the motherboard.

1. Get the latest BIOS update.
2. Go to BIOS with F1 and then click F7.
3. Go to *Advanced*.
4. Disable everything in *Platform Misc Configuration*.
5. Go to *System Agent Configuration* and select *DMI/OPI configuration*.
6. Change *DMI Max Link Speed* to Gen2.

7. Go back and select *PEG Port Configuration.* Set everything to Gen2 and *PCIe Spread* to Auto.
8. Go back to Advanced, select *PCH configuration*, then select *PCI Express Configuration*. Set *PCIE Speed* to Gen2.

That's it. You're done with the Motherboard configuration setup. Now just plug in all the GPUs, RAM, processor, SSD and connect the power supply. After this, install the mining software and you're ready to go.

Chatper-7: Future of Cryptocurrency Mining

Cryptocurrencies have a smaller user base compared to regular fiat currencies. But as technology improves and more infrastructure and awareness are created around the world, the impact of cryptocurrencies is inevitable and immense.

Venture Capitalists have invested more than 1 Billion dollars into the blockchain technology itself. This is an indication of the scope of development that is bound to occur in this field in the upcoming future. Below is a graph showing the increase in number of user-wallets of bitcoin's blockchain.

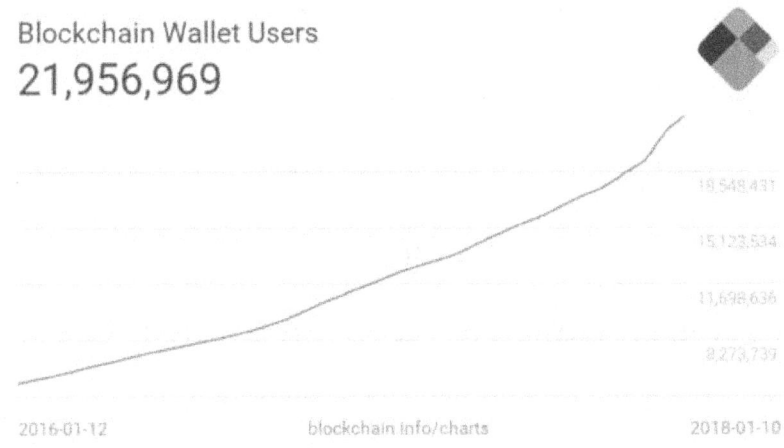

Is it all just a big bubble?

Many people ask this question when they see the market prices plunge up/down. One of the biggest arguments people make in this regard is, "Well, if it's decentralized, who's going to back it up?" There is no central authority backing up the system. So, it is easy to fall into the trap of thinking that cryptocurrencies are just treading on thin ice and have no solid ground to stand on.

But this couldn't be farther from the fact. What gives, say, Bitcoin, its value is its huge user base and widespread acceptance. If you think about it, that's what gives anything value – Public acceptance. Not centralized government backing. If you take a commodity like an Apple iPhone and ask the question "Why is it worth what it's worth?" the answer will be the same. IPhones are not backed by the government the way fiat currencies are. They are just products made by a company that people have come to assign great value to, over time. So, cryptocurrencies get their value the same way an iPhone gets its value. Public acceptance. The more they're used by the people, the more they're worth.

With cryptocurrencies, it is almost certain at this point that the total market cap will reach $1Trillion within the next 5 years. We are currently at a total of around $584 Billion. With the amount of progress being made in this field, even with a temporary value-drop or a bubble-pop, the rise of cryptocurrencies and blockchain technology is inevitable. So, brace yourselves for what is to come. Having said that, if you follow some of the tips & strategies mentioned in previous chapters, diversify your portfolio and use common sense, you will be sure to have a long and prosperous journey.

There are more and more cryptocurrencies coming into the market every month. As time goes on, we will see a range of cryptocurrencies offering different services for users. Bitcoin being the first one out there, will have an initial head start in terms of user adoption. But with all the latest innovations and the attention being paid to this space, it is difficult to predict whether bitcoin will be overtaken by other cryptocurrencies or not. Bitcoin currently occupies nearly 50% of the total market share of cryptocurrencies. Given the rising popularity of new cryptocurrencies, this situation may eventually change. But having been first to the market and being the reserve cryptocurrency to almost all other coins, Bitcoin will most likely hold the #1 position in the upcoming future.

The advent of new cryptocurrencies will be paralleled by an emergence of new crypto-exchanges. So, it will get easier for merchants and buyers to transfer the money and convert between two cryptocurrencies.

Having said this, I think we need to look at both sides of the coin (no pun intended). One of the biggest problems facing the mass adoption of cryptocurrencies is their lack of scalability. Bitcoin, for example, has had a huge growth in the number of transactions being carried out. The graph below, sourced from Wikipedia, shows how the number of transactions has been growing every year. But here's the catch – The block-size in Bitcoin is limited to 1MB. So, any blocks bigger than this are rejected by the network. This has resulted in limiting the number of transactions per second that can be processed by the network to three. To counter this limit, bitcoin miners have opted to upgrade the software so that the block-size can be increased to 2MB. This will increase the transaction fee but reduce the congestion in the network.

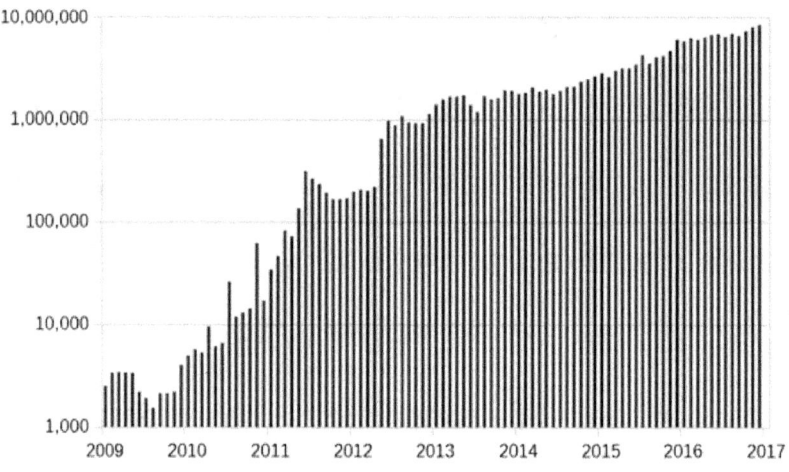

Bitcoin also had a bear market crash in the past (July 2017) where it's value dropped by around 20% in a 7-day period. Although the value is back up again, it would be foolish to believe that the cryptocurrency market is not volatile. It is highly advised for anyone interested in investing into cryptocurrencies or anyone that has already done so, to follow the latest updates and stay informed.

The Changing Landscape of Global Finance

With features like lower latency of transactions and reduced transaction fee, cryptocurrencies (especially bitcoin) have a potential for disrupting the e-commerce industry as well. The current online payment methods that users have to rely on for purchasing stuff online have lousy user experience, charge more per transaction and take longer to process payments. This gives cryptocurrencies like Bitcoin an opportunity to replace the traditional methods and create positive impact.

Due to its decentralized nature, Bitcoin has been facing restricted compliance from the banks and financial organizations. Its value dropped quite a bit when China banned Bitcoin from being used within its borders. But with blockchain, it's a different story. Financial institutions are showing positive response to the possibility of embracing the public ledger system. The reason for this seems to be the increase in operational efficiency created by using the blockchain technology.

Cryptocurrencies also seem to be advantageous for third-world countries that have underdeveloped financial infrastructure. These countries can bypass the need for spending a lot of tax money into public banks, mints and other regulatory financial organizations by directly adopting global cryptocurrencies like Bitcoin. What we're looking at is actually the possibility of unifying the world's currencies.

Although we may have new protocols for achieving distributed consensus, the participation of miners is necessary to ensure the blockchain stays up-to-date and secure. Many platforms like easyMINE are popping up to support and serve cryptominers because the efficiency of the blockchain depends on the efficiency of the miners.

To optimize the mining process, one needs access to cheap electricity, fast internet and cool climate. In the past, many miners set up shop in China because all the 3 criteria were satisfied. However, latest initiatives by the Chinese government have turned the tide and made it very inconvenient for miners to progress. So now, people have started considering India as a favorable prospect. This could also turn out to be beneficial to the Indian economy as more and more mining companies and crypto startups begin setting up shop.

There are a lot of experiments being conducted in this space and despite all the hype, cryptocurrencies are still in their early stages. So, there is absolutely no need for you to feel like you're missing out on the party. Cryptocurrencies and blockchain have the potential to change not only the payment industry but also the way business is done. With widespread decentralized distributed digital currencies, there would be no need for separate national fiat currencies. All countries around the world could fall back on a single platform of value exchange. If it happens, this will be a landmark achievement in the history of human progress. Although we have a long way to go before achieving that stage, it is quite obvious that the future of cryptocurrencies and blockchain is very bright indeed.

A few final words

Congratulations! You've made it to the end. Hopefully, it's been a fun and educational experience. I've certainly had a blast preparing this book for you. And once again, I want to express my deepest gratitude to you for having given me your time and attention. I hope you found great value worth your investment. If you did, I want you to just do this ONE thing for me.

Please leave an honest review on Amazon at the link below. That is the only way for me to get your feedback and improve my craft. Thanks a ton!

www.bookstuff.in/cryptomining-review

More from the author

Blockchain: The Technology Revolution behind Bitcoin and Cryptocurrency

Cryptocurrency Investing: The Ultimate Guide to Investing in Bitcoin, Ethereum and Blockchain Technology

Bitcoin: The Digital Gold

Cryptocurrency: The Essential Guide to understanding Bitcoin, Blockchain & More

www.ingramcontent.com/pod-product-compliance
Lightning Source LLC
Chambersburg PA
CBHW050304230526
45471CB00005B/2018